NO GOOD DEED

Matt Pelfrey

I0139752

BROADWAY PLAY PUBLISHING INC
224 E 62nd St, NY, NY 10065
info@broadwayplaypub.com
www.broadwayplaypub.com

NO GOOD DEED
© Copyright 2015 by Matt Pelfrey

Cover photo by Anthony Masters

I S B N: 978-0-88145-635-6

First printing: November 2015

Book design: Marie Donovan
Page make-up: Adobe Indesign
Typeface: Palatino
Printed and bound in the U S A

The world premiere of NO GOOD DEED was produced by Furious Theatre Company at (inside) The Ford from 21 January–26 February 2012. The cast and creative contributors were:

JOSH JAXON .... Nick Cernoch
BRYANT FELD .... Shawn Lee
DANNY DIAMOND .... Troy Metcalf
with: .... Adam Critchlow, Brian Danner,
Katie Marie Davies, Stephanie Demetriades,
David C Hernandez, Dana Kelly Jr, Danny Lacy,
Johanna McKay, Robert Pescovitz

Directed ....Damaso Rodriguez
Fight choreography ....Brian Danner
Sets .... John Lacovelli
Costumes ....Christy Haupman
Lighting ....Dan Weingarten
Video projections ....Jason H Thompson
Sound & original score ....Doug Newell
Original graphic illustrations ....Ben Matsuya

CHARACTERS & SETTING

Actor One: JOSH JAXON

Actor Two: BRANDON, SPIDER

Actor Three: DANNY DIAMOND/SECURITY GUARD

Actor Four: BRYANT FELD/FIREMAN

Actor Five: MEDIA VULTURE #1 (F) DANIELLE, MARS, AGENT

Actor Six: MEDIA VULTURE #2 (F) TALK SHOW HOST, LINDA

Actor Seven: MEDIA VULTURE #3 (M) LAWYER, MR. PRUITT, SENATOR WATSON, NIGHTMARE LETTERMAN, NIGHTLINE HOST, VAGRANT, DREW, LENO

Actor Eight: MEDIA VULTURE #4:(M) AGENT BOYLE, RON, VAGRANT, KYLE, GUY, HELLBOUND HERO, KRANK

various voices, including ALEX *and* PAUL

Time & Place:

The present.

Many locations, hinted at by light and sound.

Staging should be continues and fluid.

Feel free to start the actions of a scene before the previous scene has ended.The rear of the stage is dominated by panels that should be suggestive of comic book panels, but not literal.

A FEW NOTES:

All "hero" outfits are suggested by the eye masks and/ or found items as noted in the script. No spandex. Ever. No capes. Ever. Style is not camp, though there will be dark humor everywhere. The anti-camp note applies to sound effects and music as well. Think Frank Miller's *Dark Knight*—not the old *Batman* T V series or the train-wreck the Clooney *Batman* became. More graphic novel and animé than bright colorful comic book. All violence should be brutal and real—even when it's energy blasts causing it. Melting eyeballs hurt. Also, punches should be thrown close to full speed with no attempt to make the punches look like they land on an opponent. Punches thrown fast should be "sold" by the reaction of the character being hit. Not worrying about timing issues allows the person getting blasted to throw themselves back and react in spectacular fashion. When more than one character is fighting, audience focus will be pulled and the illusion of a raging brawl should take place. This is in contrast to the violence and beatings in the reality based scenes.

Also: Any reference to flying or big budget effects are wish-list in nature. The same effects can be done in an equally kick-ass way, yet in a cost-effective and creative manner.

Dedicated to the memory of Richard Jewell,
a hero America didn't deserve.

PART ONE

1.

(Darkness)

(Then, suddenly a red burning "H" sears across the heavens. Police sirens. Flashing lights.)

(Then, of course— The MEDIA VULTURES *descend.)*

MEDIA VULTURE #1: Maria Rodriguez *live* downtown where the strange and sad story of boy hero Josh Jaxon came to a shocking end—

MEDIA VULTURE #2: The bizarre and tragic events are finally coming into focus. Police Officers found the bodies of—

MEDIA VULTURE #3: After a city-wide manhunt, Josh Jaxon was found near the abandoned train station, the very site where—

MEDIA VULTURE #1: One year earlier to the day—

MEDIA VULTURE #2: One year earlier—

MEDIA VULTURE #3: To the exact second—

MEDIA VULTURE #1: When his heroic deed—

MEDIA VULTURE #3: His truly astounding show of courage started his—

MEDIA VULTURE #1: Sad and violent decent—

MEDIA VULTURE #2: Pathetic fall—

MEDIA VULTURE #3: Disturbing drug-fueled spiral—

MEDIA VULTURE #1: His gut-wrenching tumble into the abyss—

(The shadow of a powerful figure looms…)

(The MEDIA VULTURES see it and, frightened, slink back to the edge of the stage.)

(The powerful figure steps into the light and is revealed to be just a scrawny high school student named JOSH JAXON.)

(The burning "H" dissipates.)

MEDIA VULTURE #1: One year, to the day, when it all began.

MEDIA VULTURE #2: As a student at Central High.

2.

(JOSH wears scruffy jeans, black boots, a green army surplus jacket. His hair is a tangled, dyed-black mess. Hecsits in the high school lunch quad with a big sketch pad working on a drawing.)

(His only buddy BRANDON looks on.)

BRANDON: Bigger.

JOSH: They're bigger than her head!

BRANDON: So?

JOSH: It ain't realistic!

BRANDON: Who's cash are we talkin' about here?

JOSH: The issue's my artistic integrity.

BRANDON: I'm commissioning the drawing, correct? SO! —When I want Wonder Woman having hot— VERY HOT—and EXPLICIT—yet also sensual— lesbian sex with Super Girl—

JOSH: —right, okay, okay—

BRANDON: —and my key requirement is that they both have enormous titties—

JOSH: Yes— Got it!

BRANDON: —that's what I want, and I'd prefer it without all the fuss and backtalk.

(JOSH *sketches a bit more, finishes the picture.*)

JOSH: Here: Jugs bigger'n nature intended.

BRANDON: Oh, yes. *Nice.* Very nice. *(Beat)* This is going directly above my bed.

JOSH: Spare me the gory details.

BRANDON: Good for a solid two weeks of *vigorous* spanking.

JOSH: Just puke me some cash, freak.

BRANDON: A pleasure supporting the arts.

JOSH: Uh, you're short.

BRANDON: That's a *ten*, genius.

JOSH: Super hero porn's *twenty* per.

BRANDON: Um, yeah, for freshmen…

JOSH: Bidness is bidness.

BRANDON: Either way, ten's all I got, so—

JOSH: Owe me then. That's gonna be a collector's item.

BRANDON: Smoke another bowl.

JOSH: Be bigger than Frank Miller.

BRANDON: And I'll be power forward for the Lakers.

JOSH: Oh, dude of little faith: Feast your eyes on this. *(He digs into his backpack and pulls out a wildly illustrated manuscript.)* Finished last night.

BRANDON: No way.

JOSH: Hellbound Hero: Volume One.

BRANDON: *(Takes it, flips through it)* Ho-shit, man...

JOSH: Sell it to Darkhorse, becomes a smash, Hollywood'll buy the rights and Gullermo DelTorro does the movie...

BRANDON: ...seriously rocks.

JOSH: And don't worry, man. I'm bringing you up with me. You can run one'a the divisions of my media empire.

BRANDON: Very kind, but I'm gonna have an empire of my own.

(JOSH suddenly distracted. We see why when DANIELLE appears in a panel.)

BRANDON: Oh, give it up man. Right now. *Give* that shit *up*.

JOSH: She's fine as hell.

BRANDON: And totally outta your league. You need a starter chick. Someone *chunky* and just... I dunno... *devoured* by acne. No! I got it! You need *Leticia Villaro*.

JOSH: That's *mean*, man—she's missing *her entire jaw*.

BRANDON: I'm only *sayin'*...

(DANIELLE steps from the panel, finishes her call. She sees JOSH and waves.)

BRANDON: I did *not* just see that.

(JOSH sort of waves back.)

JOSH: I sit near her in math.

BRANDON: *Dude*, she's *coming over*...

JOSH: Be cool...

BRANDON: *You* be cool.

JOSH: *Maintain.*

(DANIELLE walks up.)

DANIELLE: *Hey* Josh.

JOSH: Hey.

DANIELLE: What's up?

JOSH: Nothin'.

DANIELLE: Cool.

JOSH: Hanging.

DANIELLE: Sweet.

JOSH: What's up?

DANIELLE: Ready for fifth?

JOSH: Can't figure that shit out.

DANIELLE: Class sucks.

JOSH: Trig's bullshit.

(DANIELLE sees Hellbound Hero.)

DANIELLE: That's cool...

BRANDON: It's his comic book.

JOSH: *Graphic novel.* Big difference.

DANIELLE: Dude, I love this stuff. All the Dark Knight and X-Men...

JOSH: Yeah, those are great.

DANIELLE: Can I?

(DANIELLE takes it. Looks it over. BRANDON and JOSH trade looks.)

DANIELLE: This is really cool.

JOSH: Thanks.

DANIELLE: I can't believe you can draw like this.

JOSH: Lots of time to practice during trig.

DANIELLE: You gotta draw me something.

JOSH: Yeah?

DANIELLE: Would you?

JOSH: Like just draw you a picture?

DANIELLE: Or whatever.

BRANDON: He draws sweet female figures.

(Awkward. JOSH *shoots* BRANDON *a look.)*

DANIELLE: I got Shankman for art. I like, took art for the easy "A", and I actually got a warning card cause I'm failing.

JOSH: You can't fail art.

DANIELLE: I know, right? I was fine with the fruit bowl stuff, but every human form I draw looks disfigured.

BRANDON: Elephant Man was disfigured.

DANIELLE: You don't say?

BRANDON: His *testicles* were literally the size of *bowling balls.*

JOSH: This is *Brandon* by the way.

BRANDON: Hi.

DANIELLE: Hey.

BRANDON: Wazzup?

DANIELLE: You should give me some pointers some time.

JOSH: Yeah, that'd be cool. Whatever's good. You know…

DANIELLE: Cool.

(The energy runs out of the convo.)

DANIELLE: Well. See ya fifth.

JOSH: Yep.

DANIELLE: Later.

*(*DANIELLE *exits.)*

BRANDON: Holy *shit*.

JOSH: What?

BRANDON: She talks like a *real person*.

JOSH: You expected grunts and whistles?

BRANDON: She treated you like a *human being*.

JOSH: Twisted, I admit.

BRANDON: I was at *half-mast* the whole time.

JOSH: Don't worry, *no way* she noticed.

(A small milk carton rockets from off stage and beans JOSH *in the head.)*

JOSH: Ah! *Damn!*

*(*DREW *and* KYLE, *two seniors enter smirking.)*

KYLE: Anyone see where my milk went?

JOSH: What's your fuckin' prob, man?

KYLE: Faggy little bitches.

*(*KYLE *shoves* JOSH. JOSH *jumps at* KYLE *but is quickly caught in a headlock.* BRANDON *steps to intervene, but* DREW *grabs him and shoves him back.)*

DREW: Get the fuck outta here.

*(*BRANDON *scrambles to his feet and runs off.)*

JOSH: Leggo!

KYLE: Make me, *puss.*

JOSH: Eat shit and choke on it!

KYLE: How about *you* eat the shit. *(To* DREW, *nods towards the rest rooms)* Dude, d-up!

*(*DREW *and* KYLE *grab* JOSH, *kicking and yelling, and carry him into—)*

(The boys bathroom)

JOSH: Fuckin' let go man let me go—

KYLE: Drop some stank 'fore we dunk his ass.

(DREW *laughs at the idea, goes to the can, drops his pants and sits.*)

(JOSH *makes another break for it,* KYLE *punches him in the stomach.*)

(JOSH *slumps to the bathroom floor.*)

KYLE: Teach you a lesson. *(To* DREW*)* Hurry up already. *Grunt* me something.

DREW: Tryin'.

KYLE: *Push,* bitch!

DREW: I'm *dry.*

KYLE: You're a *shit* machine!

DREW: I'm outta amo!

KYLE: Eye of the tiger, man!

(DREW *tries.*)

DREW: *(Stands, pulls up pants)* Nadda.

KYLE: *(Re:* JOSH*)* C'mon!

(DREW *and* KYLE *grab* JOSH *and hoist him head first above the crapper.*)

JOSH: Please, *okay,* whatever you want—don't! *Don't!* Helllllllp!

(*One of the rear panels glows red. A shape appears inside, hellishly backlit.*)

(DREW *and* KYLE *dunk* JOSH*'s head into the toilet, keeping it there a long, dangerous amount of time. Finally, they pull him out.*)

(JOSH *sputters and gasps for air.*)

JOSH: …Someone…help me….

(HELLBOUND HERO *steps out of a rear panel. Gothic, intimidating, has a sort-of Marilyn Manson feel. Most of his garb is black leather. White skin. Two huge, ragged "H"s on* HELLBOUND HERO's *chest are the dominant image…that and his red eyes.)*

DREW: Looks like he can take some more.

*(*DREW *and* KYLE *kick* JOSH *with brutal glee.)*

HELLBOUND HERO: Stop.

*(*DREW *and* KYLE *turn, see* HELLBOUND HERO *for the first time.)*

KYLE: What the…

DREW: …Whoa…shit…

HELLBOUND HERO: Step away.

*(*DREW *and* KYLE *just stare.)*

HELLBOUND HERO: STEP AWAY.

DREW: Who *the hell* are you—?

HELLBOUND HERO: Who the hell am I? WHO THE HELL AM I???

KYLE: Yo, get the *fuck* back freak—!

HELLBOUND HERO: *WHO THE HELL AM I???*

*(*HELLBOUND HERO's *wrath makes the stage glow red as he moves in on* DREW *and* KYLE.*)*

(With sudden viciousness, HELLBOUND HERO *plunges his fist deep into* KYLE's *chest and rips out his heart.)*

*(*KYLE *crumples to the floor.)*

*(*HELLBOUND HERO *tosses the still beating heart to* JOSH. *He catches it awkwardly.)*

JOSH: Uh…

*(*DREW *backs away in shock.)*

JOSH: What about *that* dick?

(Just as DREW *gets his wits together and turns to run,* HELLBOUND HERO *gestures—a sizzling burst of light engulfs* DREW—*)*

*(*DREW'*s hands go to his face and he screams horrifically, then flops to the ground and writhes in agony.)*

JOSH: What're you doing?

HELLBOUND HERO: Boiling his eyes.

JOSH: For *reals?*

HELLBOUND HERO: He'll die. Eventually.

JOSH: This is so fucking…so Fucking….*awesome!*

*(*HELLBOUND HERO *turns to leave.)*

JOSH: Wait up!

*(*HELLBOUND HERO *stops.)*

JOSH: *(Re: the heart)* Uh, what'm I supposed to do with this?

HELLBOUND HERO: Whatever you want. *(His trademark line:)* I'll see you in hell.

JOSH: Not if I see you first.

(An explosion of hellfire light and HELLBOUND HERO *vanishes.)*

*(*JOSH *takes in the carnage for a moment, then walks to the toilet.)*

(Lights tighten on JOSH *and the commode.* DREW *and* KYLE *have vanished.)*

JOSH: Told ya not to fuck with me. *(He drops* KYLE'*s heart in with a plunk. He flushes the toilet with his foot. He laughs darkly..a little bit of craziness in there, like they knocked him silly and he's still out of it…then— He collapses on the bathroom floor, unconscious.)*

DREW: *(V O)* Uh…he ain't moving man.

(Lights widen: DREW *and* KYLE *stare down at* JOSH— *they are completely whole and healthy.* KYLE *lights a joint, takes a drag.)*

DREW: Maybe we kept his head under too long.

KYLE: Wake up, Aquaman.

*(*DREW *kicks* JOSH.*)*

*(*JOSH *suddenly coughs and sputters, then turns over…and starts the same crazed kind of laugh he was doing when he flushed the heart.)*

JOSH: …told you
not to fuck…
with
me…

KYLE: Little punk's fine.

*(*JOSH *weakly holds out a hand as if shooting an energy blast. Nothing happens)*

DREW: Maybe we off'd some brain cells.

*(*DREW *and* KYLE *exit. Beat.* JOSH *struggles to his feet.)*

3.

(Two televisions click on. One plays a junk news show while the other plays some kind of reality show, or American Idol *rip off.)*

(After a moment or two, lights fill out to reveal JOSH'*s house.)*

*(*JOSH'*s mom* LINDA *and her husband,* RON, *sit at the dinning room table watching separate televisions.)*

RON: Look at this *dumb* asshole.

LINDA: *Hon…*

RON: Thinks he's gonna meet a twelve year-old he was talking to on-line.

LINDA: Ron!

RON: Pervert's gonna get the *surprise* of his life.

LINDA: Wait for my commercial—

RON: —You *gotta* see this.

LINDA: —Please?

RON: *Idiot* brought *flowers*. Why'd a twelve year-old want flowers? I mean, bring a Snickers or some Gummy Bears.

LINDA: When I'm on commercial and your show's still going, I'm not talkin' the whole time', am I?

RON: Actually, *yeah*, you are!

LINDA: No!

(JOSH enters, back pack slung over his shoulder, makes a B-line for his room.)

RON: Yo… C'mere a sec.

JOSH: Hey, mom.

RON: I said, "hold up".

(JOSH ignores RON and moves into a separate pool of light.)

(JOSH's room. There's a wall of his drawings portraying various versions of HELLBOUND HERO.)

(JOSH immediately clicks on his C D player. Some overblown rock anthem by My Chemical Romance blasts out at excruciating decibels.)

(A moment later, RON bursts in, yelling. We can't hear him. He walks over and turns the stereo off.)

JOSH: What the hell, man? Get outta here!

RON: *Where* is it?

JOSH: Where's *what*?

RON: None'a your games!

JOSH: MOM, RON'S FREAKING OUT AGAIN!

(JOSH *turns the music back on.* RON *slaps it off.*)

RON: Lookit me. What'd you do with 'em.

JOSH: With WHAT? Help me out...?

RON: My *pills?*

JOSH: I didn't steal your precious drugs!

RON: Want me to toss your room?

JOSH: "Toss my room?"

RON: That's right.

JOSH: You gonna play this prison guard crap with me?

RON: You couldn't *handle* the "prison guard" crap.

(LINDA *enters.*)

LINDA: What's wrong with you two?

JOSH: Ron's trippin'.

RON: He's a thief!

LINDA: Stop screaming!

RON: He *stole* my meds.

JOSH: Did not!

LINDA: Josh?

JOSH: I *didn't.*

LINDA: Did you take his—

JOSH: Goddamn, for like, the *sixteenth time,* no.

RON: Bullshit!

JOSH: He takes 'em and forgets 'cause he's strung-out!

LINDA: Be straight with me.

JOSH: WHAT'D I JUST SAY??

LINDA: This is serious...

JOSH: —Right, his "bad back".

RON: That's right!

JOSH: His "chronic pain".

RON: Give me my *fuckin'* pills!

LINDA: Alright—Ron!

RON: No— *No more* of this shit!

JOSH: *Don't* touch that! Hey, I pay *rent* now! *(He grabs RON by the arm.)*

(RON knocks his arm away and grabs JOSH roughly by the shirt—shakes him—throws him down on his ass. From his actions, RON looks to be in perfect health.)

RON: Control him or *I* will.

JOSH: Wow, your back seems really messed up, Ron. That convict must've kicked your ass pretty bad.

LINDA: BOTH OF YOU STOP!! Jesus! Ron! Just give us a sec. Please? *Ron?*

(RON exits.)

LINDA: His condition. Some nights he can barely sleep.

JOSH: If he's so jacked up, how come he doesn't get that shit from a *real* doc?

LINDA: Don't mess this up.

JOSH: Ron's a *prize*?

LINDA: Ron's Ron.

JOSH: That's depressing.

LINDA: Don't *even* start!

JOSH: Hey, it's *your* life, right?

LINDA: You *have* them or not?

JOSH: I DON'T HAVE HIS DRUGS.

LINDA: Can't you *ever* just help me out?

JOSH: By *eating* his shit? That's *your* job. Or something like that.

(LINDA *slaps* JOSH. *A moment. He exits.*)

4.

(*Night. A hill near the old train station. Josh alone. Sips a beer.* BRANDON *emerges from the dark with a backpack and a metal bar.*)

JOSH: 'Bout time.

BRANDON: Suck it. My family's got actual dinner together. You don't know how lucky you are.

JOSH: Score?

BRANDON: Wine.

JOSH: Beggars can't be choosers.

(BRANDON *pulls two bottles from his pack.* BRANDON *and* JOSH *start to drink.*)

JOSH: (*Nods at metal bar*) What's with that?

BRANDON: My sick agenda.

JOSH: Spill.

BRANDON: I say we stop by our beloved place of learning, a little night visit...

JOSH: I don't like being there during the day, why would we—

BRANDON: We can mess with the computer lab!

JOSH: Why? Computer sci's my only good grade. Plus, you seen the night janitor?

BRANDON: Humongous dude?

JOSH: He's from Somalia or something.

BRANDON: Prob'ly killed some of our guys in *Blackhawk Down*.

JOSH: *Rad* flick.

BRANDON: Seriously.

(BRANDON *and* JOSH *are guzzling the wine.* JOSH *looks off.*)

BRANDON: Got someplace important to be?

JOSH: Seen Danielle cut across here sometimes.

BRANDON: For real?

JOSH: Got like study time with her cousin Wednesday nights.

BRANDON: You lurk in the fucking dark, watching Danielle walk home?

JOSH: Minding my own business I saw her one time and—

BRANDON: Right—right! You stroke while you watch don't you?

JOSH: No.

BRANDON: You devious little psycho.

(*Silence. More slugs of wine*)

JOSH: Tell ya…if I was like, some dude who discovered he's got wicked-ass mutant powers—

BRANDON: Like an X-Man…

JOSH: First thing I'd do…go down my *shit list*.

BRANDON: Yeah?

JOSH: *Total* payback.

BRANDON: Which power would you have?

(JOSH *thinks. Closes his eyes. Takes another huff, then starts to float up into the sky. He hovers there.*)

JOSH: Fly. *Definitely.* I'd fly and have super strength. Those're the basics. Probably wanna like, be able to harness my cosmic energy and focus it into some *fucked up* energy blast, so I could just like gesture and *zap* the *crap* outta people. *Melt* their *skin* and *eyeballs*.

(JOSH *holds out his arms. The stage lights up as imaginary energy bolts sizzle through the air.*)

BRANDON: Nah, shit-can that.

JOSH: Yeah?

BRANDON: *Stretching* ability. Like Plastic Man or Mr Fantastic? Wrap your mind around *that* for a sec. Playing Halo in one room, my dick all *stretched* into another room *sexin'* some hot babe at the *exact same time*. How cool'd that be? Total multi-tasking.

(*A scream.* JOSH's *fantasy is shattered—he falls back down to earth with a thud. They look at each other like: What the fuck? Another scream. Desperate. Frightened. Raw*)

JOSH: Over there!

BRANDON: The station—?

(*Another scream.* JOSH *moves in that direction.*)

JOSH: C'mon—

BRANDON: *(Overlap)* Wait—

JOSH: *(Overlap)* C'mon, we gotta—

BRANDON: *(Overlap)* I'll call the cops, I'll get the—

JOSH: *(Overlap)* No, we have'ta—

BRANDON: I'm coming, I'm getting the, the—the—911—

(BRANDON *fumbles for his cell.* JOSH *grabs his metal pipe and runs towards the screaming. Lights shift to—*)

5.

(The abandoned train station. A large VAGRANT *accosts* DANIELLE.*)*

VAGRANT: *(Overlap)* Shut the fuck up shut the fuck up SHUT the FUCK UP!!

DANIELLE: *(Overlap)* GET-OFF-ME-GET-THE-FUCK-AWAY!!!

*(*JOSH *enters, freaked-out, but trying to hold it together.)*

JOSH: …Hey… *(Louder)* Hey! Get…get the hell—get away !

DANIELLE: JOSH!!

JOSH: —Hey! *HEY!* What're you doing??

*(*VAGRANT *punches* DANIELLE *in the face…she slumps to the dirt, stunned. He reaches into his boot, yanks out an ugly knife.)*

VAGRANT: Get outta here.

JOSH: Dude, man, leave her alone…

VAGRANT: *(Waves knife)* You *see* this?

JOSH: *(Overlap)* I'm tellin' ya man, LEAVE HER ALONE!

VAGRANT: Fucking *see* this?

JOSH: I mean it: I'll *mess* your shit up.

*(*VAGRANT *lunges at* JOSH.*)*

*(*JOSH *barely avoids being cut.)*

*(*JOSH *swings his pipe at the* VAGRANT *and misses.)*

*(*VAGRANT *is far more adept at fighting, and quickly backs* JOSH *up until* JOSH *stumbles to the ground.)*

VAGRANT: Now y'gonna see how it goes.

*(*BRANDON *appears on the other side of the room.)*

BRANDON: *Josh!!*

(VAGRANT *turns, distracted by* BRANDON. JOSH *seizes the opportunity, swings his pipe at the* VAGRANT'S *knees. Crack!* VAGRANT *howls and eats dirt.*)

(JOSH *rolls aside, gets up as the* VAGRANT *struggles to rise.*)

VAGRANT: Little runt...gonna fuck you up bad.

JOSH: Not if I fuck you up first.

(JOSH *smashes the metal bar down onto the* VAGRANT'S *skull.*)

(*The* MEDIA VULTURES *explode into action as the stage blazes with the media onslaught. a surge of voices and millions of cameras flash with brain-frying intensity. loud junk news show themes—dozens of different ones—warp and twist together.*)

(JOSH *caught in the media storm—there's a moment of recognition where he seems aware something horrible has just infected his life—but just as quickly, that moment ends and he staggers back, trying to shield his eyes from the glare.*)

END OF PART ONE

PART TWO

6.

(Lights up on famous female DAYTIME TALK HOST. *Crazed applause)*

DAYTIME TALK HOST: Hello and welcome.

(Applause)

DAYTIME TALK HOST: On today's show: Three American Heroes who've inspired millions. First hand stories of courage, valor and strength under the most intense pressure imaginable.

(Soft dramatic music. Lights shift, become equally dramatic.)

DAYTIME TALK HOST: December 14, 2011: For three grueling, heart-rending days, Baby Stacey lay at the bottom of an abandoned well in Pason, Arizona. The world's focus was on one man—firefighter Bryant Feld.

(Lights shift—)

(A small beam of light spears through the murky dark.)

(It's a light attached to the helmet of BRYANT FELD, *34, being lowered from above the stage as he works his way down.)*

BRYANT: *(Talking into shoulder mounted walkie-talkie)* Keep it going… Keep it going… *Shit…* Hold on… Stuck on something… Okay, okay… Gimme more…

*(*BRYANT *gets to the bottom of the shaft.)*

BRYANT: Okay...I'm down. *(Takes out collapsible shovel)* Gonna start diggin'.

(We hear the voice of ALEX, *another firefighter on the other end of the walkie-talkie.)*

ALEX: *(V O)* Need you to work at a fast clip, B.

BRYANT: Doin' the best I can.

ALEX: *(V O)* Starting to drizzle again.

BRYANT: I hear ya.

ALEX: *(V O)* Makes it minutes, not hours.

BRYANT: Understood.

ALEX: *(V O)* So, get off your ass, stop talking and earn your paycheck.

BRYANT: Ten-four. *(He digs.)*

*(*MEDIA VULTURE #1 *appears.)*

MEDIA VULTURE #1: Amanda Donaldson live from Payson, Arizona, where the rescue of Baby Stacey has turned dire as rain drenches the area. You'll notice the large tents built over the well and the parallel shaft, but I've been told it's almost impossible to stop water from draining into either the well, or the second shaft dug by rescue personnel.

*(*ALEX's *voice crackles over the walkie-talkie.)*

ALEX: *(V O)* Rescue One, this is Rescue Two, copy? Hey, Bryant, gimme some good news...

*(*BRYANT *appears at the bottom of the shaft. He digs frantically.)*

BRYANT: I'm gettin' there.

ALEX: *(V O)* It's pissin' down up here. Markinson wants you up. *(Long pause)* He's ready to call it. I'm sorry.

BRYANT: No.

ALEX: *(V O)* Bryant, man, the rain—

BRYANT: I'm almost through...

ALEX: *(V O)* The shaft could cave any moment...that whole thing's gonna fill with w—

BRYANT: I can get her. I can do it.

ALEX: *(V O)* You're not gonna have a say.

BRYANT: They try'n pull me up, I'll cut the cord.

ALEX: *(V O) Bryant.* You know how these things go—

BRYANT: --What I know is how *this's* gonna go. I got it! Help me here!

ALEX: *(V O)* I'll try'n get you a few more minutes. Out.

(Lights shift. BRYANT *gone.)*

DAYTIME TALK HOST: Then, it looked as if the worst had come to pass....

MEDIA VULTURE #1: With rain slamming down, the rescue of baby Stacey has been called off. Even now, fire fighter Bryant Feld is being pulled from the parallel shaft. The mood here is one of profound sadness as the realization sinks in...Baby Stacey will not be coming home. *(Beat)* I repeat...Baby Stacey will *not* be coming home. Back to you.

VOICE #1: Oh my god...

(More voices shout.)

MEDIA VULTURE #1: Tammy, Jim, hold on— There's some kind of commotion near the well... *(To camera man)* Can we get a shot of that? *(To Tammy and Jim)* Let me just...take a second here to see if we can find out—

VOICE #2: He did it!

VOICE #1: He's got her!

(Lights rise on BRYANT *as he staggers forward. He's caked in mud and holds a little bundle in his arms.)*

VOICE #1: Is she alive?

VOICE #2: Get the paramedic! *Now!*

VOICE #3: Is she okay??

(BRYANT *falls to his knees, exhausted, holds the baby's body up above his head. After a scary beat of silence, the baby lets out a cry. She's alive!*)

VOICE #1: *(Overlap)* Oh my god—

VOICE #2: *(Overlap)* It's a miracle!

VOICE #3: *(Overlap)* He did it!

MEDIA VULTURE #1: This is Amanda Donaldson with breaking News: Baby Stacey is *alive*. Baby Stacey is alive!

(An explosion of media sounds and flashes.)

DAYTIME TALK HOST: Ladies and Gentlemen, Bryant Feld.

(Applause. Heroic music)

(BRYANT *stands backlit in one of the panels. He poses dramatically.*)

(Lights shift. No longer backlit, we see he wears his firefighters helmet and jacket.)

(He walks out, waving like a pro to the audience. He removes his helmet and jacket—a stage hand takes them. He's wearing a sharp outfit underneath.)

(BRYANT *and* DAYTIME TALK HOST *hug, then he takes his seat at the row of chairs.*)

(Lights shift again. Dramatic music)

DAYTIME TALK HOST: The explosion at the Enchanted Kingdom shocked the Nation and the world. In the blink of an eye, a sanctuary of fun and frolic became a hellhole of blood and carnage when a bomb exploded under the bleachers during the Happy Time Fun

Parade. Four killed, thirteen others critically injured.
Little doubt the death-toll would've been higher—
much, much, higher—if not the quick actions of
security guard Danny Diamond.

(DANNY DIAMOND *appears. He's 32. A bit dumpy in*
posture and demeanor. He's desperately trying to grow a
mustache that is sadly, little more than peach-fuzz.)

DANNY: *(Into walkie-talkie)* Unit Two to Enchanted
Kingdom, Unit Two to Enchanted Kingdom, I've got
a suspicious device near the west bleachers. Send
a bomb squad immediately and prepare for evac.
I repeat, prepare for guest evac. Unit Two out. *(He*
tries to calm an unseen crowd.) Ladies and Gentlemen,
I need your attention! Excuse me? Hey! Everyone,
listen up! We gotta close down this end of the park.
I'm sorry, it's just temporary. Everyone, please exit in
an orderly manner… Thank you…make your way to
the exit… Don't push… Everything— Everything is
under control… Yes, we can refund your tickets, just
make your way out. We need to hurry. *(He turns from*
the evacuating crowd, looks around. Into walkie-talkie) Unit
Two to Enchanted Kingdom, west bleachers are clear
and secured. I'm leaving for the—*wait*—I've got two
kids just came out the bathrooms…. HEY!
NO! GO THAT WAY! BACK THAT WAY!! WE'RE—

(An explosion rips through the park.)

DAYTIME TALK HOST: Danny Diamond spent eight
weeks recovering from the blast. There's no question
he saved at least twenty-three lives that night. Please
help me welcome…*Danny Diamond.*

(DANNY appears in a panel, dramatically back lit, in his
security guard uniform and hat. He holds the pose as the
audience applauds.)

DAYTIME TALK HOST: Come on, Danny. Join the party.

(DANNY jogs up to DAYTIME TALK HOST. They hug.)

DANNY: My mom loves you, she watches everyday.

DAYTIME TALK HOST: That means she's watching right now?

DANNY: Oh, yeah.

DAYTIME TALK HOST: Say 'hi' then.

DANNY: Hi Mom! Love you.

(The audience "ah's". DANNY sits next to BRYANT. They shake hands. Lights shift. JOSH dramatically backlit in a panel.)

DAYTIME TALK HOST: And finally, let me introduce a remarkable young man. I'm sure you've all been following his story… It's my pleasure to introduce… *Josh Jaxon.*

(Applause)

(JOSH comes down from the panel and jogs over. DAYTIME TALK HOST hugs JOSH.)

DAYTIME TALK HOST: Not too overwhelmed are you Josh?

JOSH: Ah, no way. Well, maybe a little bit.

(Laughter. JOSH takes his seat.)

DAYTIME TALK HOST: Look at this: Our own Justice League of America.

(Applause)

DAYTIME TALK HOST: Josh: According to police, the man you fought off—Andrew Wilcox Beal, was a member of a railway gang linked to *dozens* of rapes and violent assaults along the Pacific Coast from Los Angeles to Seattle. *(Slight dramatic pause)* Take us through your *amazing* experience.

JOSH: Yeah, my buddy, Brandon, he's like my best friend, first we were just hanging out and whatever—

DAYTIME TALK HOST: —I understand you and your friend were on your way to study for a computer science test, you took a short cut and heard, just by luck, screams from an abandoned building...

JOSH: Uh...

DAYTIME TALK HOST: And as your friend scurried off like a frightened rabbit, you realized you had to save this young girl no matter what the risk to your own life...

JOSH: I wouldn't totally put it *that* way, I mean, Brandon, my pal, he's a good guy—

DAYTIME TALK HOST: Now back up: *Did* he run or *didn't* he?

JOSH: *Yeah*, but—

DAYTIME TALK HOST: So *then* you found a metal bar on the ground and *stormed* into the abandoned building... *alone...nobody* to help you... Stop me if I get any of the facts wrong...

JOSH: ...you more or less got it...

DAYTIME TALK HOST: —And you *bashed* that vicious predator in the head *again* and *again* and *again*. You stepped into the *jaws of hell* and *saved* a life. You were abandoned by your friend and forced to *dig deep* into your *soul* for the strength to face this nightmarish evil.

JOSH: Yeah. That's right. What can I say? I kicked his ass!

DAYTIME TALK HOST: *You* may not know. But I've got someone here who sure does. Ladies and Gentlemen: State Senator James Watson.

SENATOR WATSON: At the beginning of the year, the governor created "The Hero Fund." Money put aside to reward—to *thank*—outstanding citizen heroes like yourself. *(Lets that sink in)* From the citizens of this state to you—a small token of our appreciation: A check for *thirty thousand dollars.*

(DAYTIME TALK HOST hands JOSH an oversized check.)

JOSH: OH, YEAH! WICKED! HELL, YEAH, MAN! THANKS! *(He is totally juiced.)*

DAYTIME TALK HOST: And if that wasn't enough, we have one more very special guest.

(DANIELLE appears in a panel, then steps down.)

DANIELLE: Josh. I just want you to know that…I totally thank you for saving my life and rescuing me an' all that stuff. Seriously, that was so cool what you did…I mean, you're like a total super hero, y'know? So, I just wanna say thanks. Thank you, Josh Jaxon. You are so cool. *(She crosses gives him a kiss on the cheek.)*

(An explosion of media lights and sound. DANIELLE and JOSH pose for pictures.)

(Then finally: everyone but DANIELLE and JOSH disappear. They are somewhere else. Alone)

DANIELLE: But seriously, Josh. What you did…one good deed deserves another… *(She kisses him again.)*

(Media lights strobe. DANIELLE pulls JOSH to the ground as they continue kissing…)

(Fade to black)

(Two televisions click on in the dark.)

7.

(JOSH's house. LINDA and RON at the kitchen table. JOSH enters.)

JOSH: How'd I look?

LINDA: Amazing.

(RON *grunts*.)

LINDA: Oh, you were impressed. *Don't* act like you weren't.

RON: Did *I* say something?

JOSH: My manager says I might be doing Ellen next week.

LINDA: Oh. My. God.

RON: I don't get why you need a manager.

LINDA: He's *famous* Ron. Famous people *need* managers.

JOSH: What kind of car you want?

LINDA: Car…?

JOSH: Thirty thousand bucks!

RON: Gonna blow your wad on a car?

JOSH: Getting mom something better than that piece of *shit* she's driving now.

RON: You mean the one *I* paid for?

JOSH: *(To* LINDA*)* Gonna get you something good.

(RON, *clearly annoyed, exits.*)

LINDA: If it weren't for you, that girl would be *dead*. Maybe *worse*. Much, *much*, worse.

JOSH: I'm gonna shower, then head out.

LINDA: Who *knows* what that monster had planed?

JOSH: Yeah, ma, yeah…

(JOSH *exits.* LINDA *doesn't notice. In her own world)*

LINDA: She *owes* you everything: her *existence*. Every *minute* of it.

And if she has kids, *they'll* owe you *their* existence.
(Beat) Generation after generation for as long as her
bloodline lives. What you did…echoes on and on…
forever…it becomes more meaningful with every
birth…It's so…beautiful.

(Lights fade on LINDA *as* MEDIA VULTURE #1 *appears.)*

*(*BRYANT *appears in a separate light.)*

MEDIA VULTURE #1: And in other news, Fire fighter
Bryant Feld, the hero who rescued baby Stacy and
shot to national fame, may not be the knight in shining
armor he first appeared. Since the hunky hero—and
family man with five kids—became a media sensation,
half a dozen women have come forward claiming
to have been in long term relationships with Mr.
Feld, two of which, also claim he's the father of their
children. While none of this has been confirmed, one
can't help but think…were there's smoke…there's fire.

8.

(Someone's house. Party music throbs. BRANDON *walks in.
He looks awkward.)*

*(*JOSH *appears from the dark and grabs* BRANDON.*)*

JOSH: Yo, Brandon! What the *hell* man! Where you been
hiding?

BRANDON: Had shit to do.

JOSH: What's *up*?

BRANDON: Nothin'.

JOSH: I been calling…

BRANDON: Yeah.

JOSH: C'mere.

(JOSH *grabs* BRANDON *around the shoulder.* BRANDON'*s clearly uncomfortable.*)

JOSH: Check out the babes, dude. Live females that'll actually talk to me now...and more.

BRANDON: More like what?

JOSH: What do you think?

BRANDON: More like are you frontin' that you got some?

JOSH: Dude, *yes*. And it's even heavier than that. *Way* heavier.

BRANDON: How so?

JOSH: *Danielle.*

BRANDON: What d'you mean?

(JOSH *smiles.*)

BRANDON: *No* way. *(Beat, the enormity of his conquest sinks in.)* So, wait: You're like going out with her?

JOSH: I mean, she'd probably want too, but we, like, haven't put a "name" to our relationship. We haven't been talking about it like that. Plus, my sense is we're both at points in our life where big entanglements aren't what we're looking for. I'll save shit like that for when I'm a senior. Right now, I'm in my sexual prime.

BRANDON: Saw you in the mustang hauling ass.

JOSH: I call it The Raptor. We'll cruise later. Take corners at supernatural speeds. It's a rush. And speaking of speed... *(Looks around, shows* BRANDON *a stash of pills)* Feast your eyes on this... Entertainment upgrade courtesy of the Hero Fund.

BRANDON: Cool.

JOSH: But before we get too twisted, you want some, honeys?

BRANDON: Yeah, *right*.

JOSH: *Seriously*. Everything's changed. And I'm gonna help my best bud reap some of the reward. Gettin' all the signs from the keg rats over there. The tall one might even be in Junior College. You've heard about Junior College chicks right? Right? They like, *know things. (Beat)* Let's do it. I'll hook you up. What's mine is yours.

BRANDON: Nah, man, I gotta split.

JOSH: You just got here. We could only *dream* of action like this a month ago.

BRANDON: It's cool, man.

JOSH: What's *wrong* with you?

BRANDON: Later.

JOSH: You're not thinking clearly here, man: I can get you laid!

(BRANDON exits.)

JOSH: Brandon!?

(JOSH stares after BRANDON a beat, not sure what's up with his buddy. He downs some brew and lets it go. Looks around the room, heads for some hotties when a GUY bumps into him. JOSH spills his beer on himself.)

JOSH: What the *fuck*, man?

GUY: You're that guy.

JOSH: Wha—?

GUY: Hero an' all that shit.

JOSH: Whatever man *whatever*—

(JOSH moves to go but the GUY grabs his arm.)

GUY: Everyone sayin how tough you must be takin' on that big freak, but—

JOSH: Why're you bustin' my balls?

GUY: You kicked that rapists ass, you can kick *my* ass, right? Kick *my* ass. C'mon pussy, do it. You afraid, *pussy?*

JOSH: You really wanna do this?

GUY: Yeah. I do.

(GUY *slugs* JOSH. *The fight is on.* JOSH *gets his ass handed to him, but it quickly becomes silent and stylized and plays behind the following:)*

9.

(A blast of media noise)

(MEDIA VULTURE #3 *appears as the host of Nightline:)*

MEDIA VULTURE #3: As the investigation into the Enchanted Kingdom bombing has failed to turn up suspects, sources tell A B C that suspicion has now fallen onto Danny Diamond himself. At first hailed as a hero, he now stands accused of a brutal act of home grown terrorism. We have with us, former F B I Agent Barry Boyle, an expert in criminal profiling.

(AGENT BARRY BOYLE *appears.)*

MEDIA VULTURE #3: Mister Boyle, what can you tell us about the profile being used to hunt the Enchanted Kingdom bomber and how Mister Diamond may fit into it?

AGENT BOYLE: It's my understanding that Mister Diamond is obsessed with law enforcement, he tried to join the Police department, the F B I and the A T F on numerous occasions to no avail.

MEDIA VULTURE #3: Why was he rejected?

AGENT BOYLE: Physical, psychological and emotional reasons.

MEDIA VULTURE #3: Is it true he lives with his mother?

AGENT BOYLE: That's correct.

MEDIA VULTURE #3: So basically, this guy is a wannabe cop who may have planted the bomb *himself* for the express reason of finding it and becoming a hero?

AGENT BOYLE: We believe that's one possible motive.

MEDIA VULTURE #3: Is an arrest imminent?

AGENT BOYLE: The investigation is ongoing.

(AGENT BOYLE *and* MEDIA VULTURE #3 *disappear as* MEDIA VULTURE #1 *appears. Lights shift.*)

10.

(JOSH's *house*)

(JOSH *asleep on the couch, still dressed in his clothes from the night before, bathed in the eerie glow of the T V. He's banged up bad from the fight. It's early in the A M.*)

(RON *enters. He's either drinking now, or clearly has been.*)

RON: Wake up.

(JOSH *groans.*)

RON: HEY!

(JOSH *pulls himself to a sitting position.*)

RON: What're you doin' on my couch?

JOSH: *What?*

RON: My couch. *Mine.*

(JOSH *stares at* RON. RON *looks him over.*)

RON: Looks like someone wiped their *ass* with your *face.*

JOSH: I'm fine.

RON: Guess you're not the big man you think you are.

JOSH: What do you want?

RON: *Don't* talk back to me!

JOSH: I'm *not.*

RON: Make you feel good? This *funny* to you?

JOSH: Make any sense lately?

RON: Buying her a *car...*

JOSH: It was for you too! Not just—

RON: I can barely kick in *half* the rent!

JOSH: Look Ron—

RON: *(Exploding with rage)* DON'T FUCKING CALL
ME RON! *(He grabs* JOSH's *arm, pulls it behind his back.)*
When I met your mom she was nothing but a handful
of welfare checks with *three* rowdy brats, I put a
fucking *roof* over your heads—

JOSH: I know! St—AAAGGGGGGG! STOP!!!!

RON: —For the last TEN YEARS I *pissed my life away* for
this family...I get *knocked* on my *ass!* Laid off!

JOSH: Let go!!!

RON: Anyone's a hero around here...it's *me.*

JOSH: *Okay-okay...*

RON: *Who* am I?

JOSH: Ron?

RON: No. I'm the man of steel.

(Snap. RON breaks JOSH's finger. JOSH howls in pain.
RON exits.

13.

(DANNY *across from his* LAWYER. *A stack of letters in front of* DANNY.)

LAWYER: Relax—

DANNY: But they're—

LAWYER: I know, I know, and—

DANNY: But they—

LAWYER: You need to relax.

DANNY: They want me dead.

LAWYER: Right.

DANNY: Calling me a terrorist!

LAWYER: I've talked to the police…

DANNY: They spit on me!

LAWYER: It's ugly, I know, but I'm trying to—

DANNY: *On my mother!*

LAWYER: The police promise to put up a perimeter around the house—

DANNY: They're lying about me! They think I did it!

LAWYER: Take a breath. Listen to me: I've sent letters telling them they're opening themselves up to defamation suits…but the sad fact is, they have deep pockets, and if for whatever reason they decide they don't care, then they can do what they want.

DANNY: I'm not a punch line.

LAWYER: I know.

DANNY: Isn't there, there some kind of, of, like I dunno, an *injunction*? Can't you just—

LAWYER: No.

DANNY: I found that bomb!

LAWYER: I know that.

DANNY: Doesn't that matter?

LAWYER: No. Not yet at least.

DANNY: My mom…this isn't good for her. We have to do something *now*.

LAWYER: I told you, the police—

DANNY: They shout at her when she tries to leave. She's not eating, this—

LAWYER: When this is over, when you're vindicated, we'll make them pay. But honestly, the more over the line they step—the more jokes and insinuations made, the better our case.

DANNY: No settlement. I just want my record clean so I can join the force.

(Beat)

LAWYER: That's not gonna happen.

DANNY: I wanna be a police officer…

LAWYER: I'm gonna make sure you have enough money to start your own police department — or whatever you want. You see what I'm saying here?

DANNY: Wish I didn't find the bomb.

LAWYER: Now Danny—

DANNY: …Just got blown up then and there.

LAWYER: I'm pushing this as fast as I can.

DANNY: Let it go off. We all die together. Boom.

14.

(A bar. BRYANT *drinking. Not his first. He looks around, takes some pills out of his pocket has fun dropping them in his drink. Downs the whole thing He scrolls on his phone and hits dial.)*

(An AGENT *appears in a separate pool of light. She speaks into a headset.)*

AGENT: Bryant, what's up?

BRYANT: It's been a while...

AGENT: I'm about to step into a meeting, can we make this quick?

BRYANT: I was hoping for, like, an advance...?

AGENT: And advance...? On what?

BRYANT: "First Responders."

AGENT: What's that?

BRYANT: The reality show?

AGENT: —Yeah, about that: Let's save messages for when you're sober?

BRYANT: Can you fly me out there?

AGENT: Why?

BRYANT: Set up some pitches, get me in front of people—

AGENT: You know...Bryant...Not sure what you're expecting but...I've pushed you for everything I can push your for. It's been a nice little run but we're kinda past the freshness date. *(Silence)* Bryant?

BRYANT: Uh-huh.

AGENT: Listen. And I'm *serious* about this: If you save anyone else: call me.

15.

(Split scene:)

(DANNY appears in a black overcoat and sun glasses at his mother's funeral.)

(MEDIA VULTURE #1 appears somewhere else.)

MEDIA VULTURE #1: A new development in the Enchanted Kingdom bombing case. The mother of alleged bomber Danny Diamond was found dead this afternoon by neighbors. Let's go to April Lee, outside of the Diamond residence.

(MEDIA VULTURE #2 appears on location.)

MEDIA VULTURE #2: Sources close to the investigation say Mrs. Diamond's cause of death is not yet known.

MEDIA VULTURE #1: Is foul play being ruled out?

MEDIA VULTURE #2: At this time, no.

MEDIA VULTURE #1: Can you tell me if Danny Diamond is considered a suspect in his mother's death?

MEDIA VULTURE #2: I've been told he's not a suspect at this point but is a person of interest. *Extreme* interest.

MEDIA VULTURE #1: Another strange twist in the as yet unsolved Enchanted Kingdom Bombing case. More on that as the situation develops.

16.

(Night. Late. JOSH appears out of the darkness. He looks like shit. He's pounding on BRANDON's front door.)

(BRANDON steps out—)

BRANDON: Dude, you're gonna wake up my folks. What time is it?

JOSH: Late. Early. I dunno.

BRANDON: You don't look good.

JOSH: I'm between showers. *(Beat)* Just need to crash. My mom—Ron—I just can't deal. *(Shakes his pack)* Got some party supplies. *(Beat)* Just need a solid.

BRANDON: It's not a good time.

JOSH: What's that mean?

BRANDON: My parents won't go for it.

JOSH: So don't tell 'em. I'll crawl in by the garage and crash. Junior High all over again.

BRANDON: That won't fly.

JOSH: Don't do this shit to me.

BRANDON: My parents—

JOSH: Since when you give a shit about them?

BRANDON: Look…

(JOSH stares at BRANDON. A moment between them)

JOSH: After all I've done you give me this smack?

BRANDON: You made me sound like a bitch! All those shows and interviews! You're full of shit, man.

JOSH: I've let you be my sidekick and when I need a place to crash you fuck up.

BRANDON: I'm not your sidekick.

JOSH: You're my Robin. And a shitty one at that.

(BRANDON dives on JOSH. They fight. JOSH is surprised by the ferocity of BRANDON's attack and before long JOSH is thrown down and bleeding.)

JOSH: This is how it is? No worries. Think I don't got other friends? Supporters? *Fans?*

(JOSH moves away as lights go down on BRANDON.)

17.

(Late. DANNY *asleep in a chair, illuminated by his flickering television.)*

(Zesty theme music jolts DANNY *awake.)*

(Strange lights reveal NIGHTMARE LETTERMAN *talking to the audience.)*

LETTERMAN: Okay, folks, welcome back. This next guest needs no introduction—we've had a lot of fun with him over the last year but we've yet to have him here in person. Please give a warm welcome— Ladies and gentleman, Danny Diamond.

(Applause. Music. A spot blinds DANNY'*s eyes. A chair appears from the dark and* LETTERMAN *sits next to* DANNY *as if they were on his show set.)*

LETTERMAN: We finally meet. Face-to-face. Mano-a-mano.

*(*DANNY *is very confused.)*

DANNY: Mister Letterman?

LETTERMAN: Who were you expecting? Your dead mommy?

(Audience laughter)

LETTERMAN: And call me Dave for Pete's sake.

(Audience applauds.)

DANNY: Okay…Dave.

LETTERMAN: You know why we've brought you on the show tonight?

DANNY: No idea.

LETTERMAN: Because we owe you an apology. Is that alright? We've taken a lot of shots at you and…and well…I'm thinking maybe a heartfelt mea culpa is in order.

DANNY: What...?

LETTERMAN: Can we start this off with an old fashion "I'm sorry"? I mean, since they found the real Enchanted Kingdom Bomber and all...

DANNY: *They did?*

LETTERMAN: You don't watch the news much do you?

DANNY: Not lately, no.

LETTERMAN: Danny, we were all wrong. I wanna ask you, for all of us here at Late Night, for your forgiveness. You saved a lot of lives that day, you deserve our thanks, not vicious jokes and character assassination. And...well, I'm not good at this. Will you accept my apology, Danny? And actually, I'm certain I'm speaking for the entire country...will your forgive us?

(The crowd applauds. DANNY is in shock, but he smiles.)

DANNY: Yeah, sure. Of course. *(Tearing up)* Thank you, Dave. I mean it...I...

(LETTERMAN offers his hand. DANNY with a big smile. Reaches out to shake—)

(LETTERMAN pulls his hand away.)

LETTERMAN: Just kidding. You think we'd really call you up to apologize? Paul would we do that?

PAUL: *(V O)* No, Dave. Of course not.

LETTERMAN: We actually invited you here to watch you blow your brains out.

(Crowd applauds. Laughs. PAUL plays something on the synthesizer.)

LETTERMAN: Wait...I didn't...did I forget it...? *(He makes a big deal of searching around for something. Finally finds a gun)* Here it is. So, Danny, For this bit to work, you need to take this gun and stick it right under your chin, but angle it so the bullet goes into the center of your brain. Can you do that for me, Danny?

(DANNY *nods solemnly. Takes the weapon*)

LETTERMAN: You're gonna have do it right now, we're coming up on a commercial.

(DANNY *stares at the gun.* LETTERMAN *steps back to the edge of the darkness.*)

LETTERMAN: Let's not take forever, Danny. I'm doing you a favor bringing you on. You think I can't book a hundred suicidal 9-11 heroes in a second? Come on, now! *(Beat)* Would it help if we did the Top Ten?

PAUL: *(V O)* Great idea, Dave. Let's do a top ten.

LETTERMAN: Fine. From the home office, here's tonight's Top Ten List. *(Shakes the cards)* Top Ten reasons Danny Diamond is gonna kill himself tonight. *Number Ten*: He's literally got nothing better to do. *Number Nine*: He misses Mommy. *Number Eight*: He's never going to fulfill his dream of being a Law Enforcement officer. *Number Seven*: He found out Reno 911 wasn't real. *Number Six*: The fact the world thinks he's a murderer starting to "bum him out". *Number Five*: "Hello, I'm a mad bomber" no longer working as a pick-up line. *Number four*: This may be the only time he can use his gun to make the world safer. *Number three:* The only apology he'll ever get in print will be in his obituary. *Number two*: He picked the wrong day to forget his meds. And the *number one reason* Danny Diamond is going to kill himself: In the Afterlife: *No more Oprah*.

(*Wild applause from the audience as* LETTERMAN *vanishes.*)

(DANNY *alone in his chair. Just the T V's light on him. He puts the gun under his jaw and shoots himself.*)

(*More applause. Laughter*)

17.

(*In one of the panels,* DANNY *appears in silhouette, dressed in his full security guard uniform.*)

(*Somewhere else, lights rise on* BRYANT *in the front seat of his car. He drinks from a bottle. He rolls up the window. A tube runs into the car. It fills with exhaust as…*)

(*Lights rise on—*)

(JOSH *alone, in a dark, abandoned warehouse full of junk. He's been sleeping here on an old dirty mattress. He checks his pill bottles. He empties the remaining pills into his palm. He swallows the pills down. Drops the bottle*)

(*In the car,* BRYANT *slowly slips into unconsciousness and disappears in the cloud of exhaust. He dies. Moments later, he appears backlit in one of the panels.*)

(*A voice startles* JOSH.)

HELLBOUND HERO: Cold world for heroes…

(HELLBOUND HERO *appears in one of the panels.* JOSH *doesn't need to look at* HELLBOUND HERO *to talk to him.*)

JOSH: Know how many times I've had my ass kicked?

HELLBOUND HERO: Try this. (*He produces a baggy full of white powder. He throws the baggy to* JOSH.) They call it White Kryptonite. It's what makes Superman fly. Makes Spiderman climb walls.

JOSH: It can do all that?

HELLBOUND HERO: Snort a little, you'll be catching bullets in your teeth.

(JOSH *makes a line of white kryptonite on his arm and snorts it up. He* reels.)

HELLBOUND HERO: Try some more.

(JOSH *puts another line on the ground, snorts it up. He breathes rapidly, enjoy the energy in him—the effect of the drugs. He's burning up. Too hot. He rips his shirt open.*)

JOSH: Aaa! Sweating like a pig!

HELLBOUND HERO: Who are you?

JOSH: Huh?

HELLBOUND HERO: Simple question: *Who are you?*

JOSH: Josh. Josh Jaxon.

HELLBOUND HERO: Wrong. Josh Jaxon was consumed.

JOSH: I don't—then—okay, who am I then?

HELLBOUND HERO: The Hellbound Hero.

JOSH: *You're* Hellbound Hero.

HELLBOUND HERO: Not once you dig deep inside and unleash your true powers. Do it, Josh. Dig deep. YOU ARE HELLBOUND HERO.

JOSH: Yes.

HELLBOUND HERO: Become who you must become. Now. Now Josh.

(JOSH *finds a sharp piece of metal from the ground. Places the jagged end against his chest…and with a growl of pain, he carves two "H"s into his chest like a twisted version of the famous Superman "S". He smears black grease from an engine part on his face so it almost looks like he's wearing an eye mask. In short: He looks like a seriously fucked up super hero.*)

(HELLBOUND HERO *slowly vanishes as all of the above happens.*)

(*Just* JOSH *now*)

(Standing there)

(Chest a ruined mess of blood. His eyes closed)

(Silence. Then:)

(He opens his eyes.)

JOSH: Hellbound Hero...lives.

(JOSH thrusts his hands out—the stage explodes in a tremendous burst of hellfire.)

END OF PART TWO

(Intermission)

PART THREE

18.

(Night. Parking lot. DREW *and* KYLE *drinking brews, bull-shitting the night away.)*

(At the far end of the lot, JOSH *steps from the darkness. He's as he was in the last scene, in his nightmarishly improvised hero getup. His bloody chest is crusty and infected. He stands there, unsteady, staring at* DREW *and* KYLE.)

(A beat or two go by, then finally KYLE *notices him.)*

KYLE: Hey.

DREW: What?

KYLE: Check it.

DREW: Check what?

KYLE: There.

DREW: Oh, shit. *(Peers closer)* Freak show alert.

KYLE: Someone's having a rough night.

*(*JOSH *mumbles something.)*

DREW: Dick-head says what?

JOSH: Do you…
know…
who
I
am?

DREW: Fucked up?

JOSH: Hell...bound. I am...hell...bound...

Pause. Drew and Kyle trade a look.

KYLE: That's Jaxon.

DREW: Fuck no.

KYLE: No: *That's* Josh Jaxon.

JOSH: I am.
Hellbound.

(JOSH *throws a wild punch. Misses by a mile. Falls to the ground.*)

(DREW *and* KYLE *bust up.*)

(JOSH *struggles to his feet. Sways. Throws another punch. Misses*)

DREW: Shithead means business.

KYLE: Alright. If it's gonna be on, it's gonna be on.

(JOSH *tries again. Misses*)

(DREW *and* KYLE *lay into* JOSH. *After a nice brutal ass-kicking they step back.*)

(*Bloody and beaten,* JOSH *struggles to rise but only makes it to a sitting position. He aims his hands weakly at* DREW *and* KYLE.)

KYLE: This shit again.

(*But then* JOSH *falls on his back, and clasps both hands together, points them straight up into the sky.*)

(*A huge flash of light and two burning "H"s explodes across the heavens.*)

JOSH: You're fucked now.

KYLE: How you figure?

JOSH: (*Gesturing at the sky*) You don't see it?

KYLE: (*Staring up*) Guess not.

JOSH: Burning the sky.

DREW: I don't see shit.

JOSH: Proof you're the bad guys.

(A blast of thunder)

KYLE: Whoa-shit...

(Lightning crackles. JOSH laughs.)

DREW: The hell's...?

JOSH: *Exactly.*

(A blast of light)

(FIREMAN and SECURITY GUARD appear in two of the panels, dramatically backlit by crackling cosmic energy.)

(They both leap out from the panels and approach.)

(FIREMAN wears a full fireman's outfit [helmet, coat, boots, etc]. Including shades or a black eye-mask, whichever looks cooler.)

(Likewise, SECURITY GUARD is in a full uniform with wrap around shades or eye-mask. He carries a cop-style nightstick.)

(DREW and KYLE back off. SECURITY GUARD readies his club. DREW and KYLE don't need to see anymore. They turn and run.)

FIREMAN: Where's it hurt?

JOSH: Everywhere.

(FIREMAN and SECURITY GUARD help JOSH up. He's in a lot of pain.)

JOSH: Thanks.

FIREMAN: You sent the Flare. That happens, we answer.

SECURITY GUARD: That's the Code.

FIREMAN: Can you move?

JOSH: Depends where we're going.

SECURITY GUARD: Headquarters?

FIREMAN: What I'm thinking.

JOSH: You guys got a H Q?

FIREMAN: We look like amateurs?

JOSH: No.

FIREMAN: Okay then.

(JOSH *steadies himself. Takes a few deep breaths)*

SECURITY GUARD: Ready?

JOSH: Just about.

SECURITY GUARD: Let's make it fast. Those guys might come back with reinforcements.

(FIREMAN *and* SECURITY GUARD *hold their fists up, then look over at* JOSH.)

FIREMAN: Any time.

(JOSH *joins* FIREMAN *and* SECURITY GUARD, *fist up in the air.)*

FIREMAN & SECURITY GUARD: LET'S FUCK WITH CRIME!

(A burst of light and they're gone.)

19.

(Headquarters. Which is actually a dilapidated room in an abandoned building. Trash here and there. A stained mattress in one corner. An old fold-up card table. If there are windows they are dingy or papered over. It looks suspiciously like the place JOSH *crashed in at the end of Part Two.)*

(JOSH, FIREMAN *and* SECURITY GUARD *enter.)*

FIREMAN: Welcome to my Fortress of Solitude.

JOSH: You guys got the Batcave beat to hell.

(FIREMAN *and* SECURITY GUARD *take their hats and glasses/masks off.*)

JOSH: I know you guys…

FIREMAN: No shit.

JOSH: *(Points)* Danny Diamond. *(Points)* And—and you're that fire fighter—Bryant whatever—

SECURITY GUARD: You didn't recognize us?

JOSH: Not even.

SECURITY GUARD: *(Spinning to* FIREMAN*)* Told you the masks works. Masks *always* work.

FIREMAN: Who's ready for some justice juice?

SECURITY GUARD: Right here.

(FIREMAN *goes to a beat-up ice chest, takes out a six pack of beer. Hands them out, giving two to* JOSH.)

FIREMAN: One's for your face.

(JOSH *puts a cold one to his bruises.*)

SECURITY GUARD: What's your handle? I'm Security Guard.

FIREMAN: And surprise, I'm the Fireman.

JOSH: Right-right. Um. I'm Hellbound Hero.

SECURITY GUARD: I like it.

FIREMAN: Very badass.

SECURITY GUARD: They really pounded on you.

FIREMAN: You take a good beating.

JOSH: I'm used to it.

FIREMAN: We're gonna change that. Right S G?

SECURITY GUARD: Absolutely. Time to start dishing it out.

FIREMAN: *(Beat, noticing* JOSH *hasn't opened his beer)*
Something wrong with the brew?

JOSH: Just trying to get my head around all this.

FIREMAN: Nothing to get your head around. We're
heroes. We go eye-ball-to-eyeball with injustice. And
when we're not doing that, we fuck with crime.

(Beat. JOSH *takes a moment.)*

JOSH: I saw in the paper.

JOSH: *(Nods to* SECURITY GUARD*)* You shot yourself. *(To*
FIREMAN*)* You did it with exhaust fumes.

FIREMAN: Why you gotta bring the room down?

JOSH: Who—or like, *what* are you? Am I talking to
ghosts or…

(Walks up to JOSH. *Punches him)*

JOSH: Hey!

FIREMAN: Feel like a ghost to you?

JOSH: Damn, man!

FIREMAN: If you're not sure, I can hit you again.

JOSH: No, we're good… Just… Okay, you're not ghosts.
What's goin' on?

*(*FIREMAN *takes a big gulp of beer, tosses the empty into the*
corner.)

FIREMAN: Know what cosmic energy is?

JOSH: 'Course.

SECURITY GUARD: It's how the Fantastic Four got their
powers.

FIREMAN: Said he knows.

SECURITY GUARD: Sorry.

FIREMAN: You're like that but with cosmic energy. Your
bones. Your blood. Your skin. For whatever reason…

you have the ability to store up that cosmic energy. In your cells. It builds up.

JOSH: So wait: I'm a mutant?

FIREMAN: Big time.

JOSH: YES!

SECURITY GUARD: I'd love to be a mutant.

FIREMAN: You *are* a goddamn mutant. Just not the <u>right</u> kind.

SECURITY GUARD: Hilarious.

FIREMAN: Gets stranger.

FIREMAN: The men we were are dead in this reality. We've come from an alternate reality.

JOSH: How did things get so messed up here. For us. Why did you two…

FIREMAN: —kill ourselves?

JOSH: Yeah.

FIREMAN: And why are you gonna get murdered in prison?

JOSH: Run that by me again?

FIREMAN: You die in jail.

JOSH: Since when?

FIREMAN: You assault some guys over a drug deal and get sent to the slammer. You're strangled by your cell-mate.

(JOSH *just stares at* FIREMAN.)

JOSH: This shit can't be for real. Any of it. You. Me. We saved lives, man!

SECURITY GUARD: We messed up the time/space continuum.

FIREMAN: You were never supposed to rescue that girl. Security Guard wasn't supposed to find that bomb.

SECURITY GUARD: And Fireman wasn't meant to pull that girl from the well.

JOSH: They just, what, die?

FIREMAN: Bad things happen. You can't change what's meant to be. And when you do, reality gets infected. Which is where we're at right now.

JOSH: I just wait here and end up dead in jail?

SECURITY GUARD: X-Men 131.

JOSH: What about it?

SECURITY GUARD: The team goes back in time to stop the Sentinels from killing all the X-Men. They change reality by changing the past.

FIREMAN: That's right. More or less. We gotta go back.

SECURITY GUARD: And we're gonna do it with cosmic energy.

JOSH: Harnessing cosmic energy to make blasts or even pulling you guys into this world...that's one thing. But actually going *back in time*? Doesn't that take a lot more than we've got?

SECURITY GUARD: Fireman's got a plan for that too.

FIREMAN: White Kryptonite. If all three of us amp our cosmic energy on white K *then* combine our heightened energy we can create our own time portal. *(Beat)* It's just common sense.

(Pause. JOSH absorbs this. Heavy shit)

FIREMAN: Want your life back, kid?

SECURITY GUARD: We gotta make things right.

JOSH: What choice do I got?
Where do we start?

FIREMAN: Get White K. A lot of it. Tons of it. Enough to blast us back in time.

JOSH: Let's do it.

FIREMAN: Problem is the scumbags are holding it hostage. Hoarding it. Keeping it off the street. Making the price go sky high.

SECURITY GUARD: So we get to kill two birds with one stone?

JOSH: Fuck with crime and get the power powder?

(FIREMAN *nods.*)

FIREMAN: Guys ready to do the dirty deed.

SECURITY GUARD: More than.

JOSH: Let's get busy.

(*They move center stage. Fists in the air*)

ALL: LET'S FUCK WITH CRIME!

(*Blinding flash of light. They're gone.*)

20.

(*Drug house*)

(*A crew divides up the massive packages of White Kryptonite. Music plays. A T V is on. Besides* KRANK *and* SPIDER, *there's a few other thugs and a tripped-out junkie-chick [*MARS*].*)

SPIDER: Turn that shit off.

KRANK: Fuck you.

SPIDER: Trying to watch my shit here.

KRANK: Fuck that noise, man.

SPIDER: Turn it down at least.

KRANK: You shouldn't even be watchin that.

SPIDER: Good show.

KRANK: You got me worried.

SPIDER: Do *not* diss Project Runway.

KRANK: Man, it's just fashion bullshit.

SPIDER: It's intense competition.

KRANK: You gotta be fuckin lame as hell or something.

SPIDER: Fuck you. Everybody's got a clothes line now. It's how you diversify your brand.

KRANK: Except you don't got a brand.

SPIDER: Give me time. This shit here is just the beginning.

KRANK: You gonna be the next Puffy? Next Trump? Gonna have your own shirts an' shit? Cologne?

SPIDER: Something wrong with that?

KRANK: Yeah, man. Look at the way you're dressed. Who's gonna dress like you? You gotta lead by example if you want people to buy your clothes. Diddy dresses *sharp*. People wanna be like him. Nobody wants to be like you man.

(A buzzer rings.)

KRANK: Customer.

SPIDER: I know what the buzzer means.

KRANK: Relax, man.

SPIDER: I'm just saying, every time the goddamn buzzer goes off you gotta say customer like all the sudden I forgot what the fuck that buzzer means, even though we're both in here twenty-four-hours a day slinging Super K like there ain't no other meaning to life.

(The buzzer again.)

KRANK: So you gonna flap your gums or get it?

SPIDER: I'm gettin' it but I'm making a point first.

KRANK: So make your fuckin' point.

SPIDER: I just did.

KRANK: Fine.

SPIDER: Good.

KRANK: Great.

SPIDER: Fantastic.

KRANK: SO ANSWER THE GODDAMN DOOR.

(SPIDER *hits a button.*)

SPIDER: Talk.

VOICE: Lookin' for some product.

SPIDER: I have no idea what you're talking about. Identify.

VOICE: Got your name from Vance at the Seven-Eleven.

SPIDER: You a cop?

VOICE: Do I sound like a cop? Do cops come using the buzzer?

SPIDER: Yes or no bitch. You sound like a cop until you tell me you're not a cop.

VOICE: No.

SPIDER: No, what, pinhead?

VOICE: I'm not a cop.

SPIDER: Well I don't like you anyway. Fuck off. (*He goes back to the table.*)

KRANK: Why you turning down business?

SPIDER: My spider senses were tingling. Better safe than sorry.

KRANK: Won't argue with spider senses, man.

(*They continue the work.*)

(A rumble. It grows louder.)

KRANK: Fuck's that?

(The rumble grows louder and louder, lights flicker off and on.)

SPIDER: This ain't good.

(KA-BOOM!)

(FIREMAN, JOSH, and SECURITY GUARD explode through the wall.)

(A massive brawl as our heroes battle the drug dealers and the thugs.)

(The fight can and should spill into the audience. Hell, maybe even into the lobby of the theater. It's a raging, balls-out back and forth super battle with energy bursts, wild punches, characters flying across the stage. Whatever you can devise, as long as it follows the basic fight concepts of: Nothing campy. Nothing cheesy. Shocking violence mixed in with the over-the-top super hero theatrics. There should be some ebb and flow.)

(When the dust clears, KRANK and SPIDER and all their thugs are down for the count. The junkie-chick cowers in a corner.)

(Our heroes catch their breath. They're bruised, cut, bleeding, but amped.)

FIREMAN: That was a nice little scrape.

JOSH: For once I got to dish out the kick-ass.

SECURITY GUARD: We make a good team.

JOSH: Hell yeah we do.

FIREMAN: Let's pack this shit up.

(They begin to fill up two duffle bags they've brought along with White K.)

JOSH: Jesus, I'm shaking, like literally, just being near this much stuff.

SECURITY GUARD: Never had it before.

JOSH: You don't party much, do you?

SECURITY GUARD: Spent most of my time taking care of my ma.

FIREMAN: Gonna be in for a treat. *(He notices junkie-chick in the corner.)*

JOSH: We forgot someone.

(Junkie-chick looks scared.)

FIREMAN: What's your name pretty lady?

MARS: Don't do nothin' to me. I was just here because, like, I dunno, like, I just I just was hanging out I don't know any of 'em...

FIREMAN: I won't do nothing you don't ask me to do, how about that for a compromise.

MARS: Sweet.

FIREMAN: You got a pretty smile. You got a pretty name too?

MARS: Mars.

FIREMAN: Mars?

MARS: That's just what they call me sometimes.

FIREMAN: I like it.

MARS: My first name's Judy.

FIREMAN: Judy Mars.

MARS: Judy Marsdon.

FIREMAN: I'll go with Mars. What're you doing here.

MARS: I told you, I'm just...I dunno...

FIREMAN: You like to party?

MARS: Sometimes.

FIREMAN: Any of these clowns your boyfriend?

MARS: Not anymore.

FIREMAN: Wanna come back to our crib and keep us company.

MARS: Sure.

FIREMAN: Then get your little butt over here.

(MARS *walks up to* FIREMAN.)

FIREMAN: *(To* JOSH *and* SECURITY GUARD*)* We ready?

JOSH: We got the goods.

SECURITY GUARD: We're ready to roll.

(They all raise their fists up.)

FIREMAN: Sweet-thing, you better get close if you want to take the wild ride. Grab some hero and hang on tight.

(MARS *hugs* FIREMAN *from behind.)*

ALL: LET'S FUCK WITH CRIME!

(Explosion of light. They are gone.)

21.

(Back at FIREMAN*'s headquarters.)*

FIREMAN: Alright. Time t'get our kryptonite on.

(FIREMAN *makes three enormous lines of White Kryptonite. All three heroes get in front of a line, then yell in unison:)*

ALL: UP! UP! AND AWAY!

(They snort their white kryptonite. SECURITY GUARD *falls on his ass from the effect. They all react to the power coursing through their veins.)*

FIREMAN: Quality shit.

JOSH: Oh, yeah.

FIREMAN: VERY GOOD SHIT! VERY VERY GOOD SHIT!

MARS: Are we forgetting someone?

JOSH: We can't waste this. We don't wanna do all this White K ourselves, but we gotta.

MARS: You brought me all the way over here and you're not gonna share?

FIREMAN: Don't listen to him. Course we're gonna share. Come here.

(FIREMAN *makes* MARS *a line. She snorts.*)

MARS: *(Wipes her nose)* So, like, all you guys are super heroes, right?

FIREMAN: You have the privilege of partying in my Fortress of Solitude.

MARS: Hey, hold on…

FIREMAN: What?

MARS: That's where Superman hangs.

JOSH: Superman doesn't hang anywhere. He's in a wheelchair or something sucky like that.

SECURITY GUARD: No, he died. He died a while back.

MARS: Still. You might get your ass sued for calling this place The Fortress of Solitude. That's some copyright shit.

FIREMAN: Can they do that?

MARS: They can do anything. Just come up with a new name.

FIREMAN: I don't wanna come up with a new name.

MARS: You gotta.

SECURITY GUARD: How about "The Hero Hut"?

FIREMAN: How about I kick your ass?

(JOSH *does another line.*)

JOSH: How about "The Freedom Fortress"?

FIREMAN: Lame.

MARS: I got one: "The Justice Joint"?

(*They look at* MARS. FIREMAN *thinks about this, then nods.*)

FIREMAN: Justice Joint…The Justice *Joint*…huh…

Security Guard does a line.

SECURITY GUARD: I kinda like it.

JOSH: Not bad.

FIREMAN: That's it, this is now "The Justice Joint".

(*As if responding to some silent cue,* FIREMAN, JOSH *and* SECURITY GUARD *hold up their fists and yell:*)

ALL: LET'S FUCK WITH CRIME!

(*They all go in for another line of White Kryptonite.*)

(MARS *applauds this show of testosterone-fueled bravado, then goes to a boom box, hits "play". Funky tunes start to throb.*)

(*Everyone begins to dance, with various degrees of skill.* MARS *grooves, slow, funky, turning it into a bump and grind.*)

FIREMAN: Hey, guys? Gettin' crowded in here. How 'bout you two find your own Justice Joint for a while?

JOSH: You kiddin' me?

FIREMAN: Just gonna have a little fun.

JOSH: Thought we were gonna fix the time/space continuum?

FIREMAN: *After* I get laid.

JOSH: No fucking way.

FIREMAN: You'll get your turn.

JOSH: I don't want a turn. I wanna do this. We got the junk. It's in us, let's do it. Now. Right now.

FIREMAN: Jesus, alright. *(To* MARS*)* Sorry sweet thing.

MARS: I'll take a rain check.

FIREMAN: Oh, and I promise you baby, it's gonna rain hard.

MARS: We'll see.

*(*JOSH *motions them to join him, they create a circle.)*

JOSH: Put your fist out...

(They all extend their fists so they touch in the center of the circle.)

JOSH: Now, concentrate your cosmic energy at the center of the circle. Focus your mind, focus everything on creating a doorway...

(They all concentrate. Nothing happens.)

JOSH: ...come on! More! Try harder.

(They all try harder, almost vibrating with intensity. Nothing happens. They break the circle.)

FIREMAN: Shit!

SECURITY GUARD: We don't got the power.

JOSH: We snorted a mountain a' product... More than enough.

FIREMAN: And still not enough juice.

*(*JOSH *freaks.)*

JOSH: We need something else.

SECURITY GUARD: Give it up.

JOSH: We can't.

FIREMAN: I was wrong...I can't believe it...but—

JOSH: We gotta think. There's another angle.

FIREMAN: Like what?

JOSH: I don't know.

FIREMAN: It's over.

JOSH: It can't be.

FIREMAN: Sorry.

JOSH: Fuck your "sorry."

FIREMAN: Wait: Fuck *me?*

JOSH: Don't tell me that shit.

FIREMAN: Fuck me?

JOSH: I won't give up.

FIREMAN: You don't talk to me that way. I'll bust you down.

JOSH: Try it. COME ON! Fucking quitter! TRY IT!

(FIREMAN *and* JOSH *go after each other.* SECURITY GUARD *jumps between them, tries to hold them apart.)*

(MARS *kind of raises her hand.)*

MARS: I got an idea… *(Beat)* Hey, you guys?

(They settle down a bit.)

MARS: If you want an express ride you take the mainline.

JOSH: Mainline?

MARS: Pop it straight into your veins. I mean, if want the K to have a bigger effect and all…

SECURITY GUARD: No way. Not needles.

JOSH: Hold up: That could work.

FIREMAN: Sure you wanna chase the dragon, kid?

JOSH: M' sure about not dying in jail.

MARS: You can borrow my works.

SECURITY GUARD: Count me out. No way.

FIREMAN: You'll do it when we tell you to do it!

SECURITY GUARD: Stop bossing me around!

JOSH: You can't back out now! I'll inject you myself if I gotta.

(MARS *takes her ratty old purse and dumps it out on the card table. She digs through the stuff, condoms, gum, you name it…finally finds some needles.*)

MARS: Let's rock this shit.

(*They cook up the drugs,* MARS *fills the needles. They tie themselves off with whatever they can find.* FIREMAN *and* JOSH *get their own syringes.* MARS *is there to inject* SECURITY GUARD, *who can't look.*)

FIREMAN: We ready?

JOSH: Hell, yes.

SECURITY GUARD: Just get it over with…and don't make it hurt.

MARS: Okay.

FIREMAN & JOSH: Let's fuck with crime.

(*They inject. They all react. Stagger. Wince. Double up*)

FIREMAN: It happening?

JOSH: Don't know.

SECURITY GUARD: M'gonna puke…oh, God, my stomach's cramping…!

MARS: What's going back in time supposed to look like.

FIREMAN: Not…sure…wild lights, maybe?

MARS: I don't see no wild lights.

(MARS *slowly disappears as lights slowly close in on* FIREMAN, JOSH *and* SECURITY GUARD.)

JOSH: Wait…keep your heads clear…we gotta…gotta combine…remember? Combine our cosmic energy.

FIREMAN: Right.

JOSH: C'mon.

(JOSH *motions them to join him. They all stagger into the pose, try to raise their fists…they stumble into each other, can barely stand up.*)

ALL: Let's…ff…fuck…withtht…criemmmmmmmm…..

(*They all collapse. Black out. Low thunder rolls in the dark. An orange glow from somewhere. A harsh wind someplace. The hiss of energy crackling. Then nothing. Darkness*)

22.

(MEDIA VULTURE #3 *appears.*)

MEDIA VULTURE #1: Amanda Donaldson, live from Payson, Arizona, where the rescue of Baby Stacey has become dire as rain drenches the area. You'll notice the large tents built over the well and the parallel shaft, but I've been told it's almost impossible to stop water from draining into either the well, or the second shaft dug by rescue personnel.

(ALEX *appears on walkie-talkie.*)

ALEX: Rescue One, this is Rescue Two, copy? Hey, Bryant, gimme some good news…

(BRYANT *appears at the bottom of the shaft. He holds a mud-caked bundle that is Baby Stacey. She's crying.*)

ALEX: Rescue Two, we gotta call it. The rains coming. Talk to me. Do you see her?

(BRYANT *stares at the baby for a long moment, then places her back in the mud.*)

ALEX: I can't reach her. Take me up. Quick. Get me outta here. I'm sorry…I can't do it.

(BRYANT *swallowed by Darkness.* MEDIA VULTURE #2 *appears.*)

MEDIA VULTURE #1: With rain slamming down in a torrent, the rescue of baby Stacey has been called off. I repeat, the rescue attempt to extract Baby Stacey has been abandoned. Even now, fire fighter Bryant Feld is being pulled from the parallel shaft.

(*Lights rise on* BRYANT *as he staggers forward. He's caked in mud.* MEDIA VULTURES *surround him, sticking microphones in his face.*)

BRYANT: I couldn't reach her. I just…she was I I I couldn't…just was right there….and I…I'm sorry. I'm so sorry.

(*Screams of grief from the nearby parents.*)

BRYANT: I tried my best. I tried to…I tried. I tried goddamnit! I FUCKING TRIED.

(*The* FATHER *rushes to* BRYANT *and grabs him.*)

BRYANT: I'm sorry!

(*Commotion.* BRYANT *and* FATHER *are separated.* BRYANT *is pulled off stage.*)

MEDIA VULTURE #1: The mood here is one of profound sadness as the realization sinks in…Baby Stacey will not be coming home. (*Beat*) I repeat…Baby Stacey will not be coming home. Tammy, Jim, back to you.

23.

(Darkness. Ticking sounds. Flashlight in the dark. DANNY
*with his Maglight, shines it under the bleachers. We hear
laughter and music from the parade. The beam of light
finds a backpack,unzipped. Glimpse of the bomb inside. The
ticking gets louder.)*

(He steps back. His radio crackles.)

DANNY: Unit two to Enchanted kingdom, report of
suspicious device is a negative. Repeat: Report of
suspicious package is a negative. Someone's lunch.
Over and out. The parade can continue.

*(*DANNY *backs away, the ticking gets louder. He turns to
run, then— BOOM. He is blown forward. The orange glow
saturates the stage. He is on the ground. Screams. Moans
of pain. He stands. He's covered in blood. Not his own. He
scrambles to pick up his flashlight. He grabs an arm instead.
He shouts in terror. He tries to wipe the blood from his face,
it smears all over him.)*

DANNY: HELP ME! SOMEBODY HELP ME!!

*(*DANNY *swallowed by darkness.)*

24.

(Hill near train station)

*(*JOSH *holds the bottle of wine. Sways there.)*

*(*BRANDON *appears next to him.)*

BRANDON: Hey, answer me.

JOSH: Huh?

BRANDON: What kind of wicked super power would
you have?

JOSH: Which power?

BRANDON: What's your top pick?

JOSH: None.

BRANDON: Get outta here.

JOSH: Seriously. I wouldn't take one.

BRANDON: If you could be a bad-ass hero and do some wild shit and save all kinds a people, you wouldn't do it.

JOSH: Nope.

BRANDON: Why?

(A long pause. JOSH finally shrugs.)

JOSH: Not worth it.

BRANDON: What's with you—

(A scream)

BRANDON: —the hell…??

(Another scream. Desperate. Frightened. Raw. JOSH says the lines he did when he first rescued the girl, but this time there's a detached quality. BRANDON reacts the same and doesn't notice the strangeness of JOSH's behavior.)

JOSH: Over there. The building. The—

BRANDON: The station—?

JOSH: What it sounded like.

(Another scream. JOSH moves in that direction.)

JOSH: C'mon.

BRANDON: *(Overlap)* Wait—

JOSH: *(Overlap)* C'mon, we gotta.

BRANDON: *(Overlap)* I'll call the cops, I'll get the—

JOSH: *(Overlap)* No, we have'ta.

BRANDON: I'm coming, I'm getting the, the—the— 911—

(BRANDON *fumbles for his cell.* JOSH *grabs his metal pipe and runs towards the screaming. Lights shift to—)*

25.

(The abandoned train station. The VAGRANT *accosts the* DANIELLE.*)*

VAGRANT: *(Overlap)* Shut the fuck up shut the fuck up SHUT the FUCK UP!!

DANIELLE: *(Overlap)* GETOFFMEGETTHEFUCKAWAY!!!

(JOSH *enters. Drops the pipe. Watches as the assault takes place.)*

(VAGRANT *punches* DANIELLE *in the face…she slumps to the dirt, stunned.)*

(VAGRANT *rips at her clothes as she tries to fight and kick him away.)*

(VAGRANT *slaps her again. Stops ripping at her clothes. Starts to strangle her)*

(JOSH *can't take it anymore.)*

JOSH: Stop.

(VAGRANT *look at him.)*

JOSH: Get away from her. This isn't gonna happen.

VAGRANT: What're you gonna do about it little man?

JOSH: Whatever I want.

(JOSH *rips his shirt open, a la Superman, exposing his bloody double "H"'s. He slides his mask on.)*

VAGRANT: The fuck's this? *(Laughs)* I'm gonna gut you good.

JOSH: No you're not.

(VAGRANT *moves at* JOSH.*)*

(JOSH *thrusts his hands out at the* VAGRANT. *A loud crackling sound. A blast of light. The* VAGRANT *is toast.*)

DANIELLE: ...My god..you...what did you do... Thank you...thank you...

(JOSH *goes to her. Tries to help her to a sitting position. She's messed up.*)

JOSH: It's okay. It's gonna be okay.

(Thunder booms. JOSH *seems to know what's going to happen.)*

JOSH: You better go hide in the corner.

DANIELLE: Why...?

JOSH: We got company.

(FIREMAN *and* SECURITY GUARD *appear backlit in the panels. They jump down. Approach* JOSH. *They've changed.* FIREMAN *is covered in mud and grime. His face almost totally obscured in slime from the tunnel.* SECURITY GUARD *is still drenched in bloody gore. Blood on his face. His hands. They are both walking nightmares.*)

FIREMAN: What part of the plan don't you get?

JOSH: I can't do it.

SECURITY GUARD: Thanks for telling me. You think it was easy for me? Huh? YOU THINK IT WAS EASY???

FIREMAN: You gotta finish. We're connected.

SECURITY GUARD: All three of us.

FIREMAN: All for one. One for all. Come on, Josh. Finish what we came here for.

DANIELLE: What're you doing?

JOSH: No.

FIREMAN: You don't got a choice.

JOSH: We can come up with another—

SECURITY GUARD: IT'S TOO LATE FOR THAT. It's too fucking late.

FIREMAN: You don't finish this. We will.

JOSH: No. You won't.

DANIELLE: Who're you talking to...?

FIREMAN: S G?

SECURITY GUARD: Yeah?

FIREMAN: Cover me. I'm getting the girl.

SECURITY GUARD: Good as done.

(It's show time. SECURITY GUARD whips out his baton and attacks JOSH.)

(An amazing two-fisted battle takes place between JOSH and SECURITY GUARD.)

(Energy blasts)

(Struggle for the nightstick)

(Haymakers)

(Flying if possible)

(Throwing stuff)

(SECURITY GUARD gets the upper hand at some point, tries to press the nightstick down against JOSH's throat.)

(Meanwhile, FIREMAN is assaulting DANIELLE as if he was the VAGRANT.)

(Finally, JOSH defeats SECURITY GUARD. It should probably be by boiling his eyes the way the original HELLBOUND HERO did to the jock in JOSH's fantasy. Either way, it's brutal.)

(Just as FIREMAN is about to kill or permanently hurt DANIELLE, JOSH is able to intervene.)

JOSH: Step off.

FIREMAN: Not gonna happen kid.

JOSH: It can't go down like this.

FIREMAN: Be careful. A world of difference between me and S G. World of difference.

JOSH: What if we save them...then disappear? Isn't that better? We just don't take credit.

FIREMAN: Won't work. Only way is to have never done it.

JOSH: We save. And we walk.

FIREMAN: They'll find you. Fox. C N N...someone...

JOSH: No—

FIREMAN: And what about me. Coming out of that well. Should I take off running? That's a shit plan. Wouldn't work for me or S G. And it wouldn't work for you. It's hungry. It wants food. This is the only way to save ourselves. *(Beat)* Now back off. Let's save the ones who deserve to be saved.

JOSH: I can't let you.

FIREMAN: Then it's on.

JOSH: I guess so.

(Like gunslingers drawing, FIREMAN and JOSH both suddenly back up from each other and hold out their hands—)

(Wild bursts of energy)

(The stage lights up.)

(Sound effects like you wouldn't believe)

(Both men wilt from the other's assault.)

(They both blow each other back with energy blasts.)

JOSH: Last chance.

FIREMAN: For you.

(FIREMAN *and* JOSH *charge each other. A few punches then they both go for the same move, a punch to the other's chest.*)

(*A moment. They seem locked together in the struggle.*)

(*They part.*)

(JOSH *holds* FIREMAN'*s heart in his hand.*)

JOSH: I'm sorry.

FIREMAN: Me too.

(FIREMAN *holds up* JOSH'*s heart.*)

(FIREMAN *collapses.*)

(JOSH *collapses.*)

(DANIELLE *runs to him.*)

DANIELLE: …Hey…it's gonna be okay…it's…hey… Josh!? Wake up…WAKE UP!

(*Police sirens wail. Flashing lights drench the stage.*)

(*Then, of course—*)

(*The* MEDIA VULTURES *descend.*)

MEDIA VULTURE #1: Maria Rodriguez live downtown where the strange and sad story of boy hero Josh Jaxon came to a shocking end—

MEDIA VULTURE #2: The bizarre and tragic events are finally coming into focus. Police Officers found the body of—

MEDIA VULTURE #3: After a city-wide manhunt, Josh Jaxon was found near the abandoned train station, the very site where—

MEDIA VULTURE #1: One year earlier to the day—

MEDIA VULTURE #2: One year earlier—

MEDIA VULTURE #3: To the exact second—

MEDIA VULTURE #1: When his heroic deed—

MEDIA VULTURE #3: His truly astounding show of courage started his—

MEDIA VULTURE #1: Sad and violent decent—

MEDIA VULTURE #2: Pathetic fall—

MEDIA VULTURE #3: Disturbing drug-fueled spiral—

MEDIA VULTURE #1: His gut-wrenching tumble into the abyss...

MEDIA VULTURE # 2: Concluding with a crime spree involving the robbery of an alleged drug house—

MEDIA VULTURE #1: —and kidnapping the very girl he rescued on that fateful day—

MEDIA VULTURE #2: Bringing her here, the site of that original rescue—

MEDIA VULTURE #3: — only to suffer what doctors believe may have been cardiac arrest due to drug overdose—

(Tone shift. Maybe lights change somewhat.)

MEDIA VULTURE #1: In other news, a Donkey was released from a Mexican jail after five days of incarceration...

MEDIA VULTURE #2: Is Big Foot alive? Our roving reporter asks a true believer some tough questions...

MEDIA VULTURE #3: And in Boston, a teenager saved a family of four from certain death when he ran into their burning home and carried them to safety. More on this young hero's astounding bravery tomorrow on American Sunrise.

(BRYANT and DANNY appear in the panels.)

(A moment later JOSH steps into the empty panel between them. They exchange looks of understanding, maybe a nod between them, then, they hold up their fists...)

(...But don't say anything.)

(Hold)

(Then Slow fade to black until…)

(…only the burning red "H H" remains.)

END OF PLAY

www.ingramcontent.com/pod-product-compliance
Lightning Source LLC
Chambersburg PA
CBHW052208090426
42741CB00010B/2462